My State MISSISSIPPI

By Christina Earley

TABLE OF CONTENTS

A Crabtree Seedlings Book

Crabtree Publishing

crabtreebooks.com

School-to-Home Support for Caregivers and Teachers

This book helps children grow by letting them practice reading. Here are a few guiding questions to help the reader build his or her comprehension skills. Possible answers appear in red.

Before Reading:

- What do I know about Mississippi?
    - *I know that Mississippi is a state.*
    - *I know that Mississippi has many beaches.*
- What do I want to learn about Mississippi?
    - *I want to learn which famous people were born in Mississippi.*
    - *I want to learn what the state flag looks like.*

During Reading:

- What have I learned so far?
    - *I have learned that Jackson is the state capital of Mississippi.*
    - *I have learned that Natchez Trace Parkway is 444 miles (715 km) long.*
- I wonder why...
    - *I wonder why the state flower is the magnolia.*
    - *I wonder why Crystal Springs is known for its blues music.*

After Reading:

- What did I learn about Mississippi?
    - *I have learned that you can hike at Tishomingo State Park.*
    - *I have learned that the state animal is the white-tailed deer.*
- Read the book again and look for the glossary words.
    - *I see the word **capital** on page 6, and the word **parkway** on page 14. The other glossary words are found on pages 22 and 23.*

MISSISSIPPI

I live in Crystal Springs. My city is known for its **blues** music.

Crystal Springs is called the "Tomatopolis" of the world!

Mississippi is in the southeastern United States. The **capital** is Jackson.

Fun Fact: Jackson is the largest city in Mississippi.

The state animal is the white-tailed deer.

The magnolia is the state flower.

We grow a lot of cotton in Mississippi. Some of it is used to make clothes.

Fun Fact: Mississippi **produces** around 1 billion bales of cotton a year.

My state flag is red, blue, and gold. It has a magnolia in the middle.

My family and I like to watch the Biloxi Shuckers play baseball.

I like to go for drives with my family on the Natchez Trace **Parkway**. Sometimes we see deer.

Fun Fact: The Natchez Trace Parkway is 444 miles (715 km) long.

I enjoy swimming at Biloxi Beach.

I have fun with my family at Geyser Falls Water Theme Park.

Puppeteer and filmmaker Jim Henson was born in Mississippi. **Entrepreneur** Oprah Winfrey was also born in Mississippi.

Fun Fact: **Activist** Ruby Bridges was born in Tylertown, Mississippi.

I have fun eating crawfish at the annual King Cotton Crawfish Boil.